Micro Habits

101 Scientific Ways to
Enrich Your Life!

VISHWAS RAJ

PRABHAT
PAPERBACKS

Published by
PRABHAT PAPERBACKS
An imprint of Prabhat Prakashan Pvt. Ltd.
4/19 Asaf Ali Road,
New Delhi-110 002 (INDIA)
e-mail: prabhatbooks@gmail.com

ISBN 978-93-5521-436-2
MICRO HABITS: 101 Scientific Ways to Enrich Your Life!
by Vishwas Raj

Edition
First, 2023

Price
₹ 250/- (Rupees Two Hundred Fifty Only)

Printed at
Sanjay Printers, Sahibabad

Author's Note

The book "Micro Habits" that you hold in your hands right now is a complete guide on how you can significantly develop your habits by making 101 small lifestyle changes. And what's more, it does not demand too much time – merely 5 minutes, or even less would do.

You can think of dozens of ways to bring temporary changes in your life. It is quite possible that each of these ways could take only a few minutes to complete. So, where does the problem lie? You might think that you lack adequate time to think about all these ways. Well, the solution lies in utilizing the power of "Micro Habits."

The essence of "Micro Habits" is that you make a chain of effective small changes in your habits – like consuming fruits or sending a message of love to your dear ones – and develop a ritual of executing them every day.

"Micro Habits" proves effective because it saves you the tension of implementing too many changes, all at the same time. Your aim is ordinarily to concentrate on one action, which takes up about 15 to 30 minutes. A chain of tasks (or small changes) is part of this daily routine. Overall, you need to prepare a checklist of tasks and then follow it every day. This is the gist of "Micro Habits."

This book offers you 101 habits which can bring rapid and temporary improvement in your life. Moreover, you will learn how to make an easy daily routine based on a checklist which can be repeated daily. Even better than this is the fact that you will find ways in this book which will keep you inspired and concentrated, to the extent that even if you are totally consumed by stress, you will somehow manage to find time to complete these tasks uninterruptedly.

This book provides you with a daily action plan for all spheres of life like health, wellness, work and personal relationships. Contrary to other personal development guides, its content concentrates on taking action. So, instead of reading excessively publicized strategies that might be ineffective in the real world, you are provided with such information which you can implement instantly.

Contents

❑

1

Small Hinges Can Swing Huge Doors

"Small hinges can swing big doors." This quote by the American author, William Clement Stone, can teach one a lot about life.

The quote above simply means that a lot of big achievements are often the outcome of small incidents. If you apply this principle to your life, you will find that small changes can greatly benefit your business as well as your social and personal relationships.

A lot of books (including some of mine) emphasize making dramatic changes in life such as quitting smoking, exercising daily or writing for 30 minutes regularly. However, by making many small changes, you can notice a big difference in life.

For instance, let's talk about fruits. We are all aware of the positive health benefits of eating bananas, apples and oranges. These fruits are both sweet and delicious and one can have them as a casual snack. However, less than 50 per cent of people obtain the recommended fruit intake daily.

Think about this for a moment. It takes two minutes to eat fruit and you can carry it anywhere. Most people know that eating fruits is a healthy habit, but more than half of the population can't spare a few minutes from their daily routine to consider this habit. The motive of this example is not to lecture you on the magical benefits of fruits, but to emphasize that we all are aware of ways to improve the quality of our life, but often fail to implement them.

You can link this to some other small changes. I believe that you can, at this very moment, think of dozens of ways to instantly improve your life. Possibly, each of these ways would take you only a few minutes to complete. Then, what is the problem? You might think you do not have sufficient time to implement all these measures.

I feel that the solution lies in the concept which I call "Micro Habits."

You might have possibly felt that it isn't easy to include dozens of new habits in your daily routine, but what you might not have realized is that developing a single new routine is both convenient and simple. The essence of the book "Micro Habits" is that you create a series of small changes in life such as eating fruits and make it a ritual of implementing these changes on the daily basis.

"Micro Habits" proves effective because it saves you the stress of implementing too many changes, all at the same time. Your aim is simply to concentrate on one action, which takes up about 15 to 30 minutes. A chain of tasks (or small changes) is part of this daily routine. In sum, you need to prepare a checklist and then practice it every day. This is the gist of "Micro Habits."

WHO AM I?

I intend to show you that by consistent efforts to develop your habits, you can proceed towards an accomplished and satisfying life. Instead of lecturing you, I provide you with easy strategies which can be accommodated in any busy schedule of life. It has been my personal experience that the best way to bring long-term change is through developing one good habit at a time.

Though I staunchly believe in making a single progressive change at a time, I have discovered that it is possible to develop multiple changes at a time. All you need to do is to add the desired changes to your memory checklist.

It was a year ago that I experienced the benefits of "Micro Habits." At that time, I used to live an hour away from my girlfriend's place. Since she was a teacher and I needed a suitable place for my office, we could only meet each other during weekends.

Ultimately, after some time, our relationship became strained. After a lot of arguments, I realized that time or the lack of it was not the only issue here. The problem arose from her perception that throughout the week, I mostly did not bother to think about her or care to remember her even once. She told me that I could have at least sent her a sweet message to make her happy. Her rebuke provided me with the solution to our problem, and at that moment, my happiness knew no bounds.

My girlfriend's grudge made me realize that just like important things, even minor suggestions can bring significant changes in one's life. So, I decided to send her a beautiful love-laced message regularly. Almost overnight, our relationship saw a dramatic improvement. Though we now live together, I still send her a beautiful message every day.

So, what is it that I want to emphasize? All I want to say is that by adding a minute's habit to my daily routine, I succeeded in bringing quality improvement to my relationship.

Imagine bringing dozens of such habits into your life! You may bring such changes in any sphere of your life such as profession, relationship, health, organization and finances. However, all these will be possible only if you follow "Micro Habits" in your daily routine.

ISN'T THIS ALL-COMMON SENSE

The one challenge that a writer faces in writing such a book is that its subject matter seems to be simple common sense. It is possible that after reading a portion of this book, you may think to yourself, "Oh, but I already knew this." I understand that I am not the first person to tell you that eating fruit every day is a good habit or to say "I love you" to your significant other to improve your relationship.

The value of the concept of "Micro Habits" does not arise from individual habits. Most of us are already aware of what we should do to improve the quality of our life. What we are not aware of is how to create a series of easy and pursuable changes in our daily routine.

I intend to provide you with a book that will tell you how to change your habits fast and introduce an easy system to assimilate habits in your life. These are the things that the following pages of this book will acquaint you with.

After reading this book, you will understand how "Micro Habits" work and how they can benefit you. Which small changes are right for you and how you can start making them from today itself?

There's a lot to learn. So come, let's begin.

❑

2

Micro Habits: A Brief Introduction

Every person has their individual habits. Some of them are good like writing, exercising and eating fruit. While others are extremely harmful, like smoking, losing self-control and cheating on one's spouse. Interestingly, it's easy to concentrate on more significant habits and forget all the minor activities in our daily life.

Take for instance your habit of brushing your teeth every day. It doesn't take much of your time, but neglecting it may cause irreparable harm to your long-term health. Negligence in brushing your teeth could result in sore gums, tooth decay and bad breath. These ailments are both troublesome and expensive to treat, but one can keep them at bay by brushing one's teeth every day.

Brushing your teeth is not a time-consuming task and even the busiest of people in the world find 5 minutes to brush properly. Unfortunately, it is difficult to say the same about small things that can have a positive impact on our lives.

THINK A WHILE: Imagine, making some small habits a part of your daily routine such as keeping your home clean, buying flowers along with the grocery your wife buys, being polite with a stranger, examining your daily expenditure or eating leftover fruits. How much your life would improve by the inclusion of such habits? All of our lives are flooded with suggestions on how important such activities are, but in reality, how serious are we about implementing them?

Probably, not often.

The most common excuse for ignoring such habits is the time factor. Many of us think that there isn't enough time in the entire day to consider such habits. However, if you recall the example of brushing teeth, you will realize that people usually make the excuse of "limited time" because they do not deem it necessary to immediately consider the importance of small habits. You have ample time to brush your pearly teeth but are unable to include some good habits in your daily routine. Why?

I think the answer to this question stems from what we call "cognitive ability." The reality is that even our short-term memory has a certain limitation. It is said that an average person's short-term memory can conserve only seven pieces of information. So, the principle behind cognitive ability is that since you can conserve only some information, you need to depend on your long-term memory and plan your work according to your habits and established practices.

Think again about the short list of life changes. You are aware of how beneficial it would be to clean your home and be polite to the stranger you meet. We can easily forget these activities as they are not a part of our daily routine. Most people brush their teeth because this habit is associated with a relatively large routine of morning, evening and post-meal times. You do this work in a matter-of-fact manner, so it does not exert any pressure on your cognitive ability.

The purpose of "Micro Habits" is definitely not to nudge you in any way to develop a positive daily routine. Instead, my goal is to help you make an easy daily routine (by dint of organizing a checklist) that you can implement on a regular basis. By adopting this strategy, you need not worry about your cognitive ability, because all you need to do is to follow the checklist by memorizing it. You can develop even better work tactics which will keep you inspired and committed. So, you will find the time and energy to practice these habits regularly, even when you are stressed out.

You will find that implementing small changes can make a remarkable impact on your life. Recall the quote, "Small hinges can swing huge doors." By implementing dozens of small habits daily, you will be able to advance your business on the road to progress. These habits will help you to strengthen personal relationships, improve your financial status, get organized and improve your health.

"How do we go about it?" Before giving any further information about "Micro Habits," it is necessary to briefly clarify this question.

❑

3

Small Changes vs. Mini Habits

Some time ago, international bestselling author, Stephen Guise, authored a brilliant book called "Mini Habits: Smaller Habits, Bigger Results." Its main purpose is to show how to maintain a big habit of writing or getting things done by starting with some "small silly" writing while setting a very simple goal. The purpose of small habits is to stay committed. Commitment is much more important than what we gain from our daily habits.

Stephen gives the example of what he called "one push-up challenge." Stephen had faced difficulty in the past in sticking to his pre-determined daily routine of exercise because he had tried to cram in a year's worth of workouts into one workout. This "feasting or fasting" perspective made him hollow and deprived him of all motivation.

One day, Stephen decided to do just the opposite. He fixed the aim of doing only one push-up. It was easy as he had completed his daily quota of exercising. However, he pumped out 14 more. Then, he followed it up with one pull-up. This again inspired him to do more. He did the same in the case of sit-ups. This is how, by fixing an easy target, Stephen was able to do a substantial amount of exercise.

The main idea behind the concept of mini habits was that by starting with small activities, in the beginning, you can gradually develop bigger habits. Most people don't need much motivation to do a single push-up. So, it is easy to begin and once you start you will find you can easily keep doing them. To develop big habits like exercising, productivity, health or relationship; you can implement the concept of mini habits. If a task can develop into a big daily activity, it qualifies as a mini habit.

The small changes that I am about to discuss can be differentiated from mini habits only by their degrees of capability.

Let us consider the example of brushing of teeth again. This is one small change that all of us need to make, but you do not have a way to add any other alternative to your daily routine. You will either brush your teeth or you won't.

The same principle applies to most of the habits enumerated in this book. Each one of them is a beneficial task. If you settle on some of the habits and practice each for a few minutes, you are bound to get optimum results.

Now that you have understood the main principle behind “Micro Habits,” let us discuss the desired elements of a successful “Micro Habits” daily routine.

❑

4

8 Elements of "Micro Habits" Daily Routine

The title "Micro Habits" does sound like a puzzle, doesn't it? The aim of chaining habits together is to do more in less time which can bring positive changes in your life. As you keep doing these hierarchical activities daily, they gradually become part of your daily routine.

The nature of "Micro Habits" might seem a bit misleading at first glance. So, it is important to discuss each element of this concept. Reviewing each element will help you in understanding the concept better, which in turn will help you to develop your personal habits, make a new daily routine and bring small and positive changes in your life.

Element 1: Each habit takes less than 5 minutes to complete

According to "Micro Habits," it takes less than 5 minutes for each habit to be completed. This means that each goal is simple and does not involve a large time commitment. Once you have completed practising a particular habit, you can move on to the next habit.

Five minutes comprise merely 0.35 per cent of your day. This means you need only one-third of one per cent of a day's time to develop a habit, which will result in beneficial and long-term changes. A great example of a quick one-minute habit is to collect all your loose changes and add them to a change jar, or to write a message to a friend with whom you have not been able to connect in recent years.

Element 2: It is a complete habit

A complete habit is an action that can't be created. For example, exercising is a habit which can be formed. Exercise can change over time. It can be increased, decreased or developed. According to "Micro Habits," it has no point. Every habit is a complete task, which you can complete in very less time – you can complete a task by the time you arrange your bed. These habits are uniform daily tasks to be done every day and there is not much difference in the time taken to complete the tasks.

Element 3: These habits improve the quality of life

“Micro Habits” are designed with the intent of bringing positive changes in your life. These positive changes could be seen in any one of the following seven areas. These areas are productivity, relationship, finance, organization, spirituality, mental wellness, health, physical wellness and leisure.

This book lists 101 mini-changes which will improve the quality of your life. For instance, habits related to finances will help you remain mindful of balancing expenditure, savings and budget building. All these factors have been divided into special and pursuable daily routines.

Element 4: These habits are easy to complete

Since every habit takes less than 5 minutes to complete, it is only natural that none of these habits is complex or painstaking. The simplicity of each habit will motivate you to complete it and move on to the next habit, follow a daily routine and bring positive changes rapidly and skillfully.

You need to take some small steps to complete each habit. A simple example of this is to block retail e-mail newsletters which are computerized newsletters. This task can be achieved quite easily by following some easy steps, each of which requires merely a few seconds.

Element 5: It takes less than 30 minutes

If you chain all the fast tasks together, you can complete the "Micro Habits" daily routine in only 15 to 30 minutes. If you are new to this, you need to start by concentrating on those habits which consume only 15 minutes. This will help you avoid excessive fatigue and will ensure the completion of all your habits.

With 15 minutes routine, it is possible for you to complete anywhere between three to thirty mini-habits. In case you want to add some new habits to your daily routine, it is important to complete your routine within 30 minutes. If you make a routine of more than 30 minutes, you might take too long and might find it difficult to complete every habit on your list.

Element 6: It follows a logical process

Your "Micro Habits" daily routine should be like a constantly functioning machine. You should be able to complete each of your tasks while moving from one room to another rapidly and continuously. If you take intervals between tasks, you would end up wasting both your time and energy. This will create hurdles in the completion of your entire routine.

The entire process, like a chain of production, should continue uninterrupted until all the habits are completed.

You must complete your routine every time so that it becomes easier to follow and you get used to it, which will result in the form of positive life changes over the next few weeks or months.

Element 7: It follows a checklist

“Micro Habits” is neither a guessing game nor can it be done immediately on a day-to-day basis. It needs to be done daily in sets in an ensemble-like sequence. The best method of executing it would be to make a written checklist of habits. This way you will always remember what you need to do next and each time you do a task according to the checklist, you would get a sense of satisfaction.

Other than helping a person to get more organized and increase his productivity, a checklist does a lot more. Atul Gawande’s “The Checklist Manifesto” is the most widely-read book on how to improve personal productivity. This book will provide you with great insight and inspiration in making your “Micro Habits” checklist.

Element 8: It makes your life active and energetic

It is important to mention in this context that you should prioritize your daily routine. Concerning your habits, you should take advantage of your location and time of the day. You are usually the most energetic during the first half of the day, which means this is the time you are most alert to complete the habits that inspire and excites you.

A good example of this would be to send an inspirational story or quote to your dear ones. The selection of an appropriate topic and receiver requires vigour. However, this habit is highly rewarding and fills you with good thoughts right at the beginning of the day so that you can carefully implement the other habits in your daily routine.

It's good that you are by now acquainted with all important elements of "Micro Habits." Make sure you keep all these elements in mind when making your "Micro Habits" daily routine because these elements work collectively to brighten up the positive changes in your life.

Since all the elements work collectively, you need to incorporate all of them to create an effective "Micro Habits" daily routine. A correctly-structured "Micro Habits" daily routine is the basis of constructive and valuable habits, which results in bringing positive life changes.

Now that you know how "Micro Habits" work, let me acquaint you with the small changes that are worthy of being included in one's daily routine. I have divided them into seven categories:

- Productivity
- Relationship
- Finance
- Organization
- Spirituality and Mental Skill
- Health and Physical Agility
- Rest (leisure)

Every section has some specific activities that you can relate to your day. I can guarantee you would not be interested in all the ideas. What I suggest is that you read every section and mark the elements that you find interesting.

After you have reviewed every section, I shall introduce you to the ideas which can improve the quality of your life in the form of a functional "Micro Habits" daily routine which follows an easy eight-step process.

❑

5

Productivity

Productivity is commonly the measure to know your 'Work Capacity' during a particular day. While many time-consuming habits help you to get things done, it is possible to make some small changes that will make a positive impact on your efficiency level. I agree that some of the actions might look like common sense, but if you include them in your 15 to 30 minutes of concrete daily routine, then you will notice a dramatic improvement in both the quantity and quality of your efforts. So, let us discuss the small changes that you can associate with your productivity.

1. REVIEW YOUR GOAL

Every person has some fixed goals. Big or small, all of us have some goals to achieve. Sadly, our daily hectic schedule can lead us astray. You need to review your goals. So, that you can achieve your goals, have a realistic outlook during the day and plan the tasks to be accomplished.

Action required: Write your aims and keep them in a place where you can easily find them. They could be stored in Binder or Evernote applications. Review your aims once or twice a day. Take the time to read each goal out loud and think about the specific steps that you will take to achieve it

Time needed: 5 minutes.

2. DRINK A LARGE GLASS OF WATER

Even a minor deficiency of water in your body could, other than causing headache and fatigue, have adverse effects on your concentration, short-term memory and mental activities. If you intend to enhance your productivity, you need to keep your mind highly alert. So, before beginning a task, you need to ensure that you have consumed a sufficient amount of water.

You certainly drink more than a glass of water every day. It is mandatory to drink at least 8 glasses of water every day. Honestly, this number may vary depending on your body weight and physical exertion. The key lesson here is to add sufficient water intake to your daily habit.

Action required: Drink a glass of water. Hot or cold water, both are beneficial for good health. So, drink the water of your preference. If plain water is not palatable to you, add some ice and squeeze a lemon into it. If you do not like to drink water at all, try hot or cold herbal tea instead, but do avoid adding sugar to it. Black tea or drinks containing caffeine should be avoided too.

Time needed: 2 minutes.

3. REWARD YOURSELF ON ACHIEVING A GOAL

If you work the whole day without any entertainment, you will soon get bored and lose all your motivation. To keep yourself energetic and motivated, take small intervals between tasks and have some refreshments. Such refreshment will not only help you take breaks to compensate for your faltering concentration but will also act as a carrot on a stick to give you accelerated speed and energy to complete your task.

Action required: Think of an appropriate treatment for each goal on your list. As far as the treat is concerned, it need not be a grand feast but it could be as little as a cup of coffee, a 5-minute yoga session or a leisure reading of a magazine. On completion of bigger goals, you could make plans to meet up with a friend for breakfast or purchase an item of your own choice.

Time needed: 5 minutes.

4. PRIORITIZE TASKS ON YOUR DAILY WORK SCHEDULE

Without at least a preliminary schedule, it's frighteningly easy for you to simply slide through the day and feel like you haven't achieved anything significant. You must at least prepare a list of tasks you want to accomplish during the day and prioritize them.

Action required: Make a list of all tasks you want to accomplish by the end of the day. Instead of planning a lot of things, you should be realistic.

Determine all the tasks serially in order of their importance, for instance:

- Urgent
- Important
- Important, but not time-bound
- Unimportant

Fix an estimated time limit for each task and be liberal with your estimates. Schedule each task for a particular time. Plan to do your most important tasks first. Do not forget to list the intervals. If you feel restricted by a busy schedule, then divide your tasks into morning and evening sessions.

Time needed: 5 minutes.

5. FOCUS ON YOUR THREE MOST IMPORTANT GOALS

Another way of organizing your day is to focus on your most important goals. It is easy to put in great efforts through a pre-determined schedule. Therefore, you will feel impatient if you do not complete all your work at the end of the day. Selecting the most important tasks will allow you to pay attention to every fact every day. So, do not waste your time on less important goals. If you complete your most important tasks, you will feel a sense of achievement despite not having done your work according to your schedule.

Action required: If you have already prioritized your goals, then this step should be easy. Choose the three most important tasks from your daily list or schedule which must be completed on the same day. Do not concentrate on anything else until you have completed the tasks.

Time needed: 1 minute.

6. DIVIDE YOUR GOALS INTO MANAGEABLE STEPS

Sometimes a goal seems to be so overwhelming that you don't understand where to begin. Work suffers from this confusion leading to unnecessary tension. If you spend only 5 minutes making a list of proposed tasks or projects and divide them into manageable steps, even the hardest task would seem easy and this would in turn enhance your productivity.

Action required: Think about how you can divide each task/goal on your list into small parts. For instance, you wish to write a blog post. You can divide it as follows:

- Write a title.
- Do some research.
- Create a sub-heading and outline.
- Write a post.
- Check for spelling and grammatical errors.
- Prepare a draft for the website.

- Decide on the pattern of the source and images.
- Organize the images.
- Upload and send the post.

By dividing a task into specific steps, you will have a better idea of how to prepare a task list and what is necessary for that.

Time needed: 5 minutes.

7. FOCUS ON EACH STRATEGY

There are very few who can fully concentrate on the work at hand. There are chances that you might get distracted by other projects, aims and strategies. It is futile to ignore these ideas that come to mind (Have you ever thought of ignoring them? It is impossible). So instead, jot them down or make a note of them on an electronic notepad. Once they are out of your mind as you have made a note of them elsewhere, they will be forgotten and you can concentrate on your work.

Action required: Keep an electronic notepad on the floor so that you are always prepared to jot down ideas that come to your mind. Alternatively, you may use your computer or mobile application like 'Evernote' to do the same.

Time needed: 1 minute for each idea.

8. BE COMMITTED TO THE SMALL GOALS

The toughest part of completing a task is to begin it. Naturally, the toughest aspects of a task make the mind drift towards easier and more interesting work like checking Facebook or reorganizing paperwork, among others. Once you have crossed the initial hurdle, you will then happily keep doing the task even beyond the proposed time limit.

Action required: Setting a goal as simple as writing for 5 minutes reduces the difficulty of the task in your mind and the initial hurdle goes away. This is the reason I love the simplicity of Stephen Guise's book "Mini Habits."

Action required: Think of your toughest goal and plan some small and easy steps that will take only a few minutes to ensure its completion. Choose an easy task which you know you can complete.

Time needed: 2 minutes.

9. FIX ACCOUNTABILITY BY TELLING OTHERS

No matter how careful you are in planning the details, not much good will come of it if you do not execute your plan scrupulously. When you are accountable only to yourself, you will habitually keep postponing the work, delay taking action on your goals or never complete your listed tasks.

If you have not determined any implicit accountability (like telling your customer the due date), then you must fix accountability by telling other people. This will offer a glimpse into your intention and make you disciplined enough to sincerely stick to your goal. You would definitely not relish the idea of being shamed for your inaction. So, if your aims are made public, you will work dedicatedly towards fulfilling them.

Action required: Tell someone about your productivity and work goals. You can make someone your productivity partner and both of you can be accountable to each other through discussions or by staying connected by e-mail. Alternatively, you can use the social media platform to inform people about your goals. All these steps can keep you responsible and accountable.

Time needed: 5 minutes.

10. DETERMINE TIMEFRAMES FOR DIFFERENT ACTIVITIES

Have you ever felt that you have worked the whole day, but have nothing worthwhile to show? Most people estimate the work time to be longer than the actual time taken and waste a lot of time on silly tasks. Scheduling time will make you alert to how you are spending your time. Scheduling time will help you identify the ways by which you are diminishing your productivity.

Action required: Though lots of applications are available to help you schedule time, you can easily make a note of the starting and completion time of each task.

There is a helpful software application called 'Rescue Time' which can help you determine how you are utilizing

time on your computer. This application keeps running in the background and sends a report at the end of each task which helps you to understand literally how much time you have spent on different software applications and websites. To say the least, this application can be a great eye-opener.

Time needed: If you are using a self-regulated application, you can set it and forget it. However, should you choose to make a note of the time on your own, it could take 5 minutes in a day.

11. REMOVE ALL DISTRACTIONS BEFORE STARTING WORK

Humans are too curious by nature and most people find it impossible to ignore e-mails and social media notifications until the completion of a work session. If you are distracted by a message tone or browser tab flash, it could greatly diminish your concentration and productivity.

These social activities provide immense joy. In other words, you get addicted to social media. What takes about 5 minutes to breeze through Facebook, could turn into hours due to addiction and many can vouch for this. Instead of struggling against a natural inclination to postpone work, it is better to shut down e-mails and social media during work to avoid being distracted.

Action required: If you are not interested in distractions like e-mails, shut them down before starting work. In case you want to enhance your willpower, there is such software which can stall attractive websites while you work. You may use applications like 'Stay Focused' or 'Cold Turkey' to end such attraction before you start your work.

Time needed: 1 minute.

12. CLEAN YOUR DESKTOP

If you are surrounded by the commotion, your concentration suffers. Spending 5 minutes cleaning and organizing your workplace could be as satisfying and productive as turning over the pages of your diary. An untidy desk is also distracting and constantly diverts the mind towards other things. Once you have removed these physical distractions, you are bound to notice an improvement in your concentration levels.

It is not just your physical environment that needs to be organized. Even a cluttered computer screen where you have stored a lot of files can cause distraction and you can end up wasting time searching for important files. Merely being organized will immediately raise your productivity.

Action required: Barring papers needed for the day's work, remove all other things from the desk. Put everything out of sight in physical folders, file boxes and shelves. Clear your desktop by deleting unwanted files and downloads. Put everything in precise folders.

Time needed: 3 to 5 minutes (depending on the extent of the untidiness of the desk.)

13. PLAY MELODIOUS MUSIC TO IMPROVE CONCENTRATION

Peaceful music such as rain-like or wave-like sound patterns and simple background music, like the whirring of a fan or the dim voices at a coffee shop, helps you remain concentrated towards your goals. The low-level sound of background music helps suppress a distracting sound and has been seen to improve creativity.

Action required: Experiment with different sounds to find out which helps you the most in keeping you concentrated. There are websites that store sounds like those of an air-conditioner, sounds from Nature and sounds from a busy coffee shop. There are many applications for I-phone and Android which offer you different melodious background music to choose from.

Classical, instrumental and music based on surrounding Nature are considered the best for concentration. Most people find lyrical music to be distracting. However, author Stephen King writes about the heavy metal backing track, "You may be surprised which music is most effective for you. You then need to have a look at the playlist on YouTube and Spotify posted by users of tracks that enhance productivity."

Once you have zeroed in on the ideal 'working sound,' you can play it while at work.

Time needed: 1 minute.

14. DO THE MOST DIFFICULT OR MOST BORING TASKS FIRST

When you cast a glance at the list of tasks, you would obviously be attracted to the easy and more interesting ones. If there is a big project you have at hand, there is a possibility you would put it off for later and after some time, perhaps, forget about it altogether. However, if you deviate from the league and take up the big project first, then you will have the satisfaction that it is now on top of your worklist. The rest of the tasks will feel like a breeze in comparison to it.

A study on eminent musicians suggested that contrary to expectations, instead of practising the known ragas and tunes, they deliberately focused on practising the tough ones that made their practice sessions more effective. If you look at the most difficult tasks on your worklist, you would realize that they are the most rewarding goals.

Action required: Carefully study the most important tasks on your work list and mark them out instead of postponing them indefinitely. Start working on them without thinking about them as you might then be tempted to put them aside. Do not think about working on any other task until you have completed them.

Time needed: 1 minute (for choosing the toughest tasks)

15. WORK IN SMALL PHASES

As discussed earlier, our mind is usually biased against tough tasks. What we can do is divide our work into small chunks to make them more manageable. If you sit quietly and decide that you wanted to work for three hours, your mind is likely to resist the decision and tempt you to postpone the effort. It is better to divide your work into small chunks and take an interval between two chunks of work.

This technique is best exemplified by the Pomodoro Technique, which is a time management method which allows you to work in short bursts of time with short breaks in between. According to this technique, one can take rest for 5 minutes after every 25 minutes of work. This '25-minute-work and 5-minute-break' schedule may not be suitable for all and it's best for you to first ascertain your concentration span before fixing a schedule.

Action required: Set the timer at 25 minutes (or whatever period suits you). You may use a physical kitchen watch, a stopwatch, or any other app. There are many Pomodoro timers available for Android and I-phone. You may also take help from the Online countdown timer *e.ggtimer*.

Time needed: Less than 1 minute to fix the timer.

16. USE THE 2-MINUTE RULE

We often cut off unpleasant tasks that are unrelated to our current projects, even if they only take us two minutes. In doing so, many works remain incomplete which later takes a lot of time to complete. Let's say, for instance, that you clean your plate immediately after having a meal rather than clutter your wash basin with plates with the intent to clean them at the end of the day.

Action required: If any task takes about 2 minutes or less to perform, do it immediately and move ahead.

Time needed: 2 minutes.

17. MAKE A LIST OF ALL WORK DONE

Most people are familiar with the concept of the to-do list, but if there are too many projects to be completed, then such a list would soon tire you out and rob you of all motivation. A day-to-day checklist, on the other hand, will keep you motivated.

Action required: As soon as you complete a task, make a note of it or make a list at the end of the day of all the things done. You can make this list on paper or use an app. like 'I Done This.'

Time needed: 5 minutes.

❑

6

Finance Management

In order to improve your financial status, you need to be disciplined and focused. When you think of finances, your meaningful expenditure depends on your desires. Fortunately, good financial desires do not demand too much leisure time. There are, in fact, many activities which can help you improve your financial status.

18. LIST ALL EXPENDITURES MADE IN THE PAST

Being careful about your expenditure is the best way to ensure financial management. Listing the cost of every item bought will help you gain an insight into your spending habits. You will soon be acquainted with your spending inclinations and this will in turn help you cut down on your expenditure.

Action required: Make use of a notebook or expense book to jot down all your expenditure from the previous day (yesterday). You can Instead of trying to recollect your expenditure every time, you can preserve your receipts which will make your task simpler. The cost of every item bought, inclusive of taxes, on a day, should be written. You may also mention if you paid in cash or by cheque or credit card.

Time required: 3 minutes.

19. TRANSFER OF FUNDS

It is imperative to know how much funds you own and where they are kept. If you know your funds, you can decide better how it needs to be saved and spent. Borrowing beyond your means or having your cheque bounced are costly habits and you can get rid of these habits easily.

Action required: Take note of your bank accounts and credit union accounts. Make a note of the funds in each account. Decide whether you need to transfer funds from one account to another to pay bills or for some other expenditure.

Time needed: 5 minutes.

20. PACK YOUR MEALS AND SNACKS

Packing lunch for the office or taking homemade coffee on a journey is not just a healthy option, but it is also less expensive. Going out for lunch or coffee every day is an expensive affair, while lunch or coffee can be prepared at home for only one-third of that cost.

Action required: Go to your kitchen and find out what you can pack for lunch and breakfast. Keep it near your purse or keys so that you do not forget it. Taking homemade a journey can also prove to be easy in your pocket.

Time needed: 2 minutes.

21. ACQUIRE COUPONS FOR CERTAIN NECESSITIES

There are certain necessary items that you need to buy at any cost but you do not need to overspend for each item. You can acquire items like soap and napkins by using coupons to save money.

Action required: Browse websites or go through newspapers for coupons to buy things like toilet paper, garbage bags and paper towels. Cut out the coupons from the newspaper (or take printouts from the Internet) and keep them in your purse to avail of them the next time you intend to buy such items.

Time needed: 3 minutes.

22. READ ARTICLES, LEARN FINANCIAL DISCIPLINE FROM OTHERS

One doesn't need to be well educated, especially in the matter of finance. To take a sound financial decision, one must know about the economy and personal finances. To avoid overspending and inculcate the habit of saving, one must learn from others.

Action required: Browse Google, Yahoo or Bing to search for articles on financial management. Be it advice or an article by a financial expert, you are sure to gain insight into how to manage and improve your finances.

Time needed: 5 minutes.

23. SWITCH OFF ALL LIGHTS AND DEVICES

This is the easiest way to save money. You can save significantly by switching off all lights and devices in your home, office or apartment. Since saving money this way is easy, follow it for the sake of your finances and to protect the environment.

Action required: Look around your home, office or apartment. Immediately switch off all lights and devices that are not in use.

Time needed: 2 minutes.

24. KEEP LOOSE CHANGES TOGETHER

If you are desirous of reaping the maximum benefit from the loose changes you collect, you must get into the habit of putting them all together. The more loose changes you keep adding to your change jar, the more you will keep adding to your savings account which adds up over time.

Action required: Wherever you find some extra money, be it in your pocket, purse or kitchen desk put them all in one place or a piggy bank. Stash it all away in a cabinet and forget about spending it.

Time needed: 2 minutes.

25. PLAN YOUR DAILY ACTIVITIES

Planning your daily activities is like planning your daily budget. This keeps you alert and organized. Instead of going to places which will entail more expenditure, visit places where it is more logical for you to go. Such planning will save you time, money and energy.

Action required: Make a list of all tasks that need to be completed. Then arrange the tasks in the order in which you plan to complete them. Ensure your commitment according to the list and avoid an unscheduled visit to any place. This will save you both time and money.

Time needed: 2 minutes.

26. KEEP A TAB ON YOUR CASH

When you are aware of the amount of cash you have, you can make better decisions on its expenditure. If you need to pay a bill, it is important to know how much cash you have. If you need to buy something from a shop which does not accept credit/debit cards, you need to know the amount of cash you have in hand. You often end up spending more if you pay by credit card and if you do not clear the credit card dues, the interest will keep piling up.

Action required: Count the money in your pockets and put it all in your purse. If you need to pay for anything in particular, like lunch or bills, keep some money aside for the concerned purpose.

Time needed: 2 minutes.

27. STAY AWAY FROM WORTHLESS E-M[illegible] AND CATALOGUES

E-mails that promise discounts and printed catalogues often unnecessarily hike our expenditures. A discount of ₹ 20 on something that costs ₹ 100 is not a discount in any case. So, steer clear of such messages and do not spend extravagantly.

Action required: Scan your inbox and overlook insignificant e-mails. Every e-mail has an 'unsubscribe' icon, but it could take a minute to find it. So, unsubscribe from such worthless emails. Do not accept any promotional material from near your home. Call up the companies who send you such promotional material that they remove you from their mailing list. Make use of services like 'Catalogue Choice' and 'Unroll Me' to make this process easier.

Time needed: 5 minutes to remove such subscriptions.

28. DO SOMETHING

You can have fun without going out of the house and spending any money but many people often ignore this fact. Dinner at a restaurant and a movie at a multiplex – both can cost you more than ₹ 100. It is better to spend this money on buying groceries or paying credit card bills. Look out for free-of-cost activities in your locality. This can help you save money and manage your finances better.

Action required: Look for free-of-cost activities in your local newspaper or website. Watch out for free programmes ganized at nearby parks. Pick out your favourites and make a note of those activities in your calendar so that you do not forget them.

Time needed: 3 minutes.

29. FIX YOUR DAILY EXPENDITURE LIMIT

If you are trying to improve your financial status, you need to keep track of your daily expenditure. Limiting your expenditure helps you to save and avoid spending more money on unimportant things.

Action required: Set a realistic amount limit for your day's expenditure. Keep a tab on your bills which need to be paid. Fix an amount which does not allow you to splurge and make unnecessary purchases.

Time needed: 1 minute.

30. COMPARE THE PRICES WHILE SHOPPING ONLINE

Comparative shopping helps you avoid overspending on essential items. It is important to compare the prices while making expensive purchases. This will help you save money and shop wisely.

Action required: Choose the items you need to buy. Look for the prices of the items on at least three websites. Look at their description, features, availability and price. Select the website that offers you standard items at the cheapest and best price.

Time needed: 5 minutes.

31. MEET SUCCESSFUL PEOPLE

Every human has flaws. No one is perfect. One who identifies his shortcomings and rectifies them in time achieves success. When you try to improve constantly, you move nearer to success. On the contrary, if you consider yourself an expert in everything and stop learning, your success will be short-lived.

To be successful you need to meet people who are more successful than you, who think and lead their lives positively. Spend as much time as possible with them. Such people will help you to develop a positive perspective, succeed in your business and find solutions to your problems. You may also read motivational books which will help you as a life coach. This way you can learn how to make progress in life.

To achieve success, you need to keep an eye on the work of successful people and ask them about how they achieved success in their sphere of work. Then, reflect on your shortcomings. If you are not aware of your strengths and weaknesses, then how can you expect yourself to improve?

Interact with those who are more successful than you. If you intend to scale the peak of success in the modern age, you need to enhance your communication skills. Always try to improve the tone of your conversation. For this, you may seek advice from successful people or join a course. Your communication skills will help you inch your way toward success.

32. CREATE YOUR VISION BOARD

A vision board is a collage of your dreams, goals, images of your desires, photographs and affirmations that make you happy. This may also be called a 'dream board.' Making a vision board can help you to realize your dreams and achieve your goals better as it will work as a source of inspiration. Actually, on the vision board, we focus on our goals. The vision board is a general description of what we want in life, our goals and the things that make us happy.

The following factors may be included while making a vision board:

- What is an ideal life from your perspective?
- How can you make your life valuable?
- What do you want to achieve in life?
- What are the things you want to learn?
- What are your hobbies?
- Are you satisfied with the things you do and do you want to improve upon them?
- What are your goals?
- What is your dream – getting a job or doing business?
- What steps do you need to take to achieve your goal? For instance, do you need a special degree or need to do an internship?
- What are your goals in your personal life?
- Do you want to be in a relationship for a long time or settle down with your spouse and kids?

- How much time do you want to spend with your spouse?
- How do you want to remember your personal life?
- How do you want to remember the happy and sad moments in your life?
- Do you intend to write your autobiography?
- Do you want to inspire people by taking charge as the president of an organization?

By creating such a vision board, you may fulfil most of your dreams.

❑

7

Spirituality and Mental Wellness

Some are very religious, while others concentrate on their mental wellness. Contrary to your beliefs, you can develop lots of habits that will keep you feeling energized and in touch with the world around you. What you are about to read are some changes you can add to your "Micro Habits" daily routine.

33. STAY IN TOUCH WITH NATURE

Nature has a peaceful and healing effect on our bodies and mind. An additional bonus is the Vitamin D which you get from the sun. It is advisable to rise early from the point of view of physical fitness.

Action required: If you do not have enough time for morning walks, you can have your tea and breakfast outside.

Before going to bed the previous night, you can keep your teapot ready, along with other materials, so that all you need to do in the morning is to boil water. In any case, you need not be a tea lover to relish the fresh morning air. If you have a garden, the best time to water the plants is in the morning or you may also take your pet dog for a walk. Try to feel the sounds, smell and scenery of the surroundings.

Time needed: 5 minutes. This is one activity that you can turn into an exercise routine by adding a little more time. But remember, you can still reap the mental benefits by briskly going around your block.

34. SPEAK WITH DETERMINATION

If you start your day positively, it could do wonders for your general behaviour throughout the day. To enhance your self-confidence, stand in front of a mirror and speak in an assertive voice and leave the house feeling empowered. A few good thoughts can greatly improve the quality of your daily routine.

I agree that this habit may seem a bit unnatural to some people. However, if you have a problem with self-confidence, then this is a simple solution to feeling happy in the coming days.

Action required: Rise as early as possible and look into the mirror. While looking in the mirror chant mantras or *shlokas* loudly. For instance, you can recite the following affirmations:

"I am in command of my life."

"People love and admire me."

"I can make a difference in the world."

"I am a generous person by nature."

"I will achieve my goal today."

Time needed: 5 minutes.

35. DERIVE JOY FROM LOOKING AT PICTURES

We are all aware of the strong impact of visualization on our beliefs. When we look at a photograph or portrait, different feelings emerge in our minds. We can rekindle the same feelings time and again by looking at the same picture.

Observe pictures that fill your heart with gratitude, joy, inspiration and positive thoughts. When you look at pictures of your near and dear ones, you re-live the beautiful and happy moments of the past, which in turn fills you with love and warmth.

Action required: Re-live the happy moments of your past through visualization. You can do this by browsing the photographs saved on your computer or mobile phone. An album of photographs can also provide the same joy. As an alternative, you can also go through these photographs on blogs and social media as per your choice. Visual nourishment is extremely interesting. All you need is to search for pictures of your interest.

Time needed: 5 minutes.

36. MAKE YOUR MUSCLE MASS FLEXIBLE

This might seem a bit funny to you, but massaging your muscles in front of the mirror can have a beneficial effect on your holistic conduct. Not everyone is in a good shape, but seeing your muscles in the mirror can make you realize your physical strength. This will also help you boost your mental strength. You will feel more in control if you realize your physical strength. The thought of being in control of your life and the feeling that you are capable of defending yourself can sharpen your physical fitness.

Action required: Look at your muscles while standing in front of the mirror. Examine them from various angles. If you follow an active lifestyle, you will notice a remarkable improvement in your muscle mass. However, if you were not careful about it before, then it would serve as a warning to you. Knowing your muscles will help you look toned during the day.

Time needed: 2 minutes.

37. MAKE A GRATITUDE LIST

Our actions stem from our thoughts. So, it is natural that we give our thoughts a definite shape through our actions. It is good to make a list of persons to whom you owe a debt of gratitude or of things that give you joy. Your list is a visual affirmation of the positive things in your life which will lead you to positive thoughts and actions.

Action required: Make a habit of keeping a 'gratitude list' beside your bed. Jot down three things that you are grateful for or three things that give you joy. For instance:

"I am grateful I am in good health."

"I am grateful I could spend time with my friend today."

"I am fortunate I could pay my credit card bill."

Time needed: 3 minutes.

38. LISTEN TO YOUR FAVOURITE SONGS

It's amazing to know what listening to your favourite song can do to your body and mind. Good music not just gives you great joy but also helps you reminisce about your sweet memories. Without your knowing, you will start dancing and singing along and thus get prepared to start your day happily.

Action required: Download or buy some songs that are close to your heart. If you have good Internet connectivity, you can tune in to online radio stations or iTunes radio. Listen to songs early in the morning while going about your daily chores.

Time needed: 5 minutes.

39. PRACTICE SPIRITUALITY

When we practice spirituality, our body becomes stale and focuses on elevated, pure and just thoughts. Both prayer and meditation keep you concentrated on a single goal which makes you realize the balance between the Self, Nature and the Almighty. Seek something that will give you peace of mind during such moments of silence.

Action required: Identify a quiet place where you would not be disturbed while you practice spirituality and make sure you are in a comfortable position. If you are not religiously inclined and do not want to pray, sit in a quiet place, light a candle and concentrate on your breathing. You will then feel energetic, calm and refreshed.

Time needed: 5 minutes.

40. READ AN INSPIRING QUOTE

You can find inspiration from the most interesting places. All of us have our own stories and incidents, which we keep close to our hearts. They may be religious or enlightening but they are extremely effective.

Action required: Search for websites or books with inspirational quotes. The following page has a whole lot of inspirational and motivational quotes – http://www-livinglifefully.com/flo/floexerpts.htm Read a single inspirational story to equip you with enough inspiration to go ahead. Do not just depend on regular quotes. Search for something new that can help you move ahead on an innovative path.

Time needed: 3 minutes.

41. ENJOY A CALMING BEVERAGE (LIKE TEA)

A hot cup of tea can inspire positive thoughts and improve your general perspective. A cup of green tea can reduce the toxicity of your body and can keep your body hydrated. Water is essential to keep you healthy. You can plan your next day's schedule while enjoying a drink and also evaluate all the tasks you have done during the day.

Action required: Make a cup of tea or coffee after you wake up in the morning and enjoy it.

Time needed: 2 minutes.

42. STRETCH YOURSELF EVERY MORNING

It is good to stretch yourself in the morning after a long night's sleep. When you stretch your muscles, it leads to better blood circulation, reduces stress, and increases balance and energy. These in turn will help you start your day on a positive note.

Action required: Stretching after taking a bath is beneficial. The muscles become soft after a hot water bath. Start with basic exercises: Touch your toes first. Then raise your hands above your head, join them and bend on both sides. You will feel your muscles stretch and your body will indicate the areas which need stretching. Do not make haste in undertaking this process and patiently determine its start and end.

Time needed: 5 minutes.

43. PRACTICE CHANTING MANTRAS

This practice could seem a little controversial to some, but chanting is all about giving voice to your positive thoughts. When you repeat certain sayings or words full of vitality, you feel empowered from within. All kinds of sounds have an impact on the body and mind. So, if you accustom your body and mind to positive sounds, it would give you a lot of peace. Proper practice of chanting mantras could help you reduce the levels of stress, anxiety and depression.

Action required: Although, it may seem silly at first, the positivity drawn from chanting mantras greatly depends on the repetition of sounds created and their pronunciation. Make a list of sayings and mantras. Have a positive attitude towards them as they can impact your life, behaviour and action. Write the mantras on separate pieces of paper and put them all in a small box. Practice chanting one mantra loudly every day.

Time needed: 5 minutes.

44. SPARE TIME TO PLAY

Think as a child how you would wake up in a mood to play. Alongside, you would think about how to become more creative and active. This mindset doesn't have to change just because you have matured or become an adult. Play time will reduce stress and bring a smile to your face. If you have children, playing with them early in the morning will increase your working capacity. The concentration levels of your children will also increase. Playing with a pet can increase blood circulation and create positive vibrations in your body.

Action required: Make a daily routine of playing with your kids, pets or friends. If there is no one to give you company, you can play some games alone on your mobile phone or Tablet. Some of these games could be addictive. So, fix yourself a time limit. Playing such games while on a journey is also a great way to pass the time. Alternatively, you can play a game of hide-and-seek with your kids or run with your pet dog near your home.

Time needed: 5 minutes (or more if you have time).

45. PRACTICE SIMPLE MAKEUP

Find a little time for simple makeup in your morning routine as it really makes a difference to your personality. If you go to your workplace well-dressed and groomed, you feel respected and confident. Outwardly too, a little self-grooming can boost your image and self-confidence.

Action required: Before leaving for work, make sure you are impeccably dressed. After grooming, apply some perfume and scented lotion. Trim your untidy eyebrows and apply some makeup. Men can use some facial cream or cologne.

Time needed: 5 minutes.

46. READ MAGAZINES AND PERIODICALS

All of us need to be aware of what's happening around us. By reading magazines, we understand our thoughts and feelings better and based on them, we can determine our actions. If you are going through a bad phase, you can know the causes and influences behind your hard times by reading articles published in magazines.

Reading magazines can help you understand and organize all that is happening in your life. Once you understand your struggles better and can analyze the situation, you can accept what you can't change with more patience and composure.

Action required: Maintain a diary. Write about your thoughts, feelings or all that's happening in your life, either at the start or end of the day. You can even include details of your meals in it as it will give you an idea of how your meals affect your thoughts and what inclines you towards emotional eating. If you are not a big fan of writing, you can jot down your thoughts in a bullet manner and also remember to determine which points are co-related.

Time needed: 5 minutes.

47. HELP AND SERVE OTHERS

If you live in a joint family or with renters, inculcate the habit of helping others. Helping others can work wonders for our well-being and when we are appreciated, we feel happy. When you help others, the negative thoughts that clog your mind are cleansed. It also boosts self-confidence and the joy that comes from helping others destroys the negativity that invades our minds.

Action required: Allowing a person standing behind you in a queue to enter a room first can be interpreted as a way to help others. At home, you can make coffee every morning for all the members of your family, collect the mail or newspaper and even offer a lift to your friend to his home or office.

Time needed: 5 minutes.

❑

8

Relationships

Relationships give meaning to our life. Be it an important person or a member of the family, a child, a friend or a close associate, it is important to work on our relationships and move ahead in our life with a positive attitude.

The truth is we often ignore our relationships in a mad rush to achieve our goals. We feel we have no time to connect with people. However, you will see how it is not too difficult to add a few relation-building activities to your daily routine.

48. PRACTICE FOCUSED THINKING

When you focus your attention on a particular task, thing or activity, it is called focused thinking. If you are focused on a minor task, it is a bit easy, while it takes more hard work, time and positive thinking to complete a bigger task.

Let's say, if you have decided to reduce your weight by 5-6 kilograms, it is an easy task, but if you have decided to clear the IAS examinations, it is a tough job. Tough, but not impossible. All you need is to work in the right direction and the right manner with focused thinking and inch your way ahead.

Stay focused on one goal at a time. It will help you to devote your time to achieving your goal and also you will be able to organize your goal properly. If you take up too many goals at the same time, then your time and preparation will get divided and focused thinking will elude you.

Focused thinking teaches you to move ahead of your past challenges. It can help you to transform past challenges so that you can deal with them patiently without being perturbed. It reduces tension and helps you to sleep better so that you are inspired to do better. Especially in the post-Covid scenario, you can manage your life better in such uncertain times.

Focused thinking also removes negativity. Pay attention throughout the day at what time your mind gets clogged with negative thoughts. This is the time when with the help of focused thinking, you can create positive opportunities for yourself. This is the way you can dust off all negative thoughts and replace them with positive ones.

49. APPRECIATION WORKS

A genuine compliment makes everyone happy and allows you to feel well about yourself too. Pleasing someone out of the blue is rewarding and it is a good way to make friends or develop a relationship.

Action required: Keep an eye on things which please you, like somebody's attire or recent achievement. If you come across a well-attired person or someone who has achieved something, appreciate them with an open heart.

Time needed: 2 minutes.

50. MAKE SURE TO ANSWER PHONE CALLS AND MESSAGES

Communication is a two-way street which leads us towards healthy relationships. If you have received a message, it is important to reply to it to maintain a relationship. Timely given replies to phone calls and messages build credibility in relationships.

Action required: First, look for missed calls. Answer the calls in the order of their sequence. Apologize for not having been able to take the call and ask the other person what you could possibly do for him. Then, answer the text messages in order of sequence. Lastly, look for unread e-mails in your inbox and reply to them.

Time needed: 5 minutes (the time could differ from person to person).

51. CONNECT TO THOSE WHO SHARE YOUR VIEWS ON SOCIAL MEDIA

Establishing relationships is only one of the reasons for connecting to social media. The second reason is to gather information about people who share the same views as you and are facing the same challenges. Whether you are undergoing training for your first marathon or are baffled by the prospect of preparing a meal plan on a fixed budget, in both situations meeting the right people who support and guide you can make a big difference in your life. Social networking accounts can transform your life.

Action required: Search for an Online forum or Facebook group which shares your habits or personal interests. Thereafter, spend a few minutes conversing with people on such a website every morning. There are many reasons why this step is necessary. Some benefits of doing this are:

You become accountable for your actions when you converse with others about your purpose.

You get connected with like-minded individuals.

You get to know about new strategies and tips for success.

Tracking your progress becomes easy.

Time needed: 5 minutes.

52. WRITE SOMETHING ENCOURAGING

Sometimes you do something for others that makes you feel good about yourself. Take a moment to write something encouraging about a 'special' someone. This is not an enormous task, but it would make you feel better about yourself.

Action required: Think about someone who needs your encouragement during the day. The person may be working on an important project, test, sport event or meeting. Write a few simple words to wish them well and let them know that they matter to you.

Time needed: 2 minutes.

53. FIX DATES FOR LUNCH OR DINNER

The best way to remain sociable is to keep your social calendar full with dates for lunch and dinner with people. To get to know someone, go out for lunch or dinner and strengthen your bonds with the person.

Action required: Call, text or e-mail a friend, family member or colleague to ask if they are available for lunch or dinner. Tell the person about a specific date, time and place for the meeting. If the person agrees to meet up, make a note in your calendar so that you do not forget about it and make other plans.

Time needed: 2 minutes.

54. SPEND TIME TO KNOW A PERSON BETTER

To know someone well and to have an exchange of ideas, it is essential to spend some time with the said person. This will help you to know about the conditions and direction of the person's life. If you start thinking from the other person's perspective, you will connect with the other person better.

Action required: If you have differences with a friend, family member or colleague, think of what others think of you. Think about this and try to do something. In trying to understand someone else's perspective, you will learn how to establish effective communication with others.

Time needed: 5 minutes.

55. KEEP TRACK OF YOUR SOCIAL ENGAGEMENTS

While planning social engagements, every event on the list must be given enough time. Do not double book to meet a person or to attend some other event. Do not engage yourself so much in social work that you can give only a minimum of time to meet people. Keeping your social calendar organized makes your life easier and makes you more responsible towards society. By making dual bookings in your schedule or being unable to give adequate time to people, your social image could tarnish and this could also spoil your relations.

Action required: Sit calmly and go through your table calendar, e-mails and phone calendar. Also, check the information on social plans written elsewhere. Take some time out to take note of new events or to acquire fresh information about dates, times and locations of pre-planned events. If you find that you have mistakenly agreed upon attending two different events at the same time or given the same time to meet two different people, then reach out to them and politely request them to meet another day. Do not forget to apologize for this slip.

Time needed: 4 minutes.

56. CONNECT ON FACEBOOK OR LINKEDIN

Connecting on Facebook or LinkedIn helps you to expand your social circle. You can get to know thousands of people on these sites every day. Many of these people might be interested to connect with you to enhance friendship or business connections and hence might send you friend requests. There could be occasions when new relationships might rekindle the memories of past relationships. So, start an invigorating and interesting conversation with your new contacts.

Action required: Log in to Facebook or LinkedIn. Both sites have a 'People you might know' section. Look for acquaintances you can connect with. If you do find such acquaintances, click the 'Add friend' or 'Connect' button.

Time needed: 3 minutes.

57. MEET A NEW PERSON

To expand your social circle, meeting a new person is an excellent way. If you remain too involved with yourself, you will never be able to make new friends. If you do not introduce yourself to others, chances are that your social life will remain incomplete.

Action required: Introduce yourself to people in your classroom, office and neighbourhood. Shake hands in a friendly way when you meet someone new and ask about their well-being. Tell the other person about your occupation and interests. Make him leave with the feeling that you were truly glad to make his acquaintance.

Time needed: 2 minutes.

58. SHARE INSPIRATIONAL THINGS

Sharing inspirational quotes, stories and blog posts with other people shows that you take time to think about them. Sharing an inspirational story or quote can strengthen your bond with a person and make both of you feel good about yourself.

Action required: Search for excellent quotes, articles or blog posts on Google or Twitter. You can send links through Google or Twitter. You can also get them printed and send them by post or even personally hand them over to a person.

Time needed: 5 minutes.

59. SHARE NOTES WITH MESSAGES

Leaving notes with messages for a friend, family member or colleague can go a long way in building strong relationships. Imagine the joy one would get on receiving such a note. This is another way to strengthen relationships. There are numerous ways to fill someone's day with joy. The person shouldn't get to know about the ways that could bring joy to his day as it would then come as a pleasant surprise to him. You could try one of these following ways: leave a note on a person's pillow, prepare the tiffin box for your kid and leave a sweet written message inside it or write an encouraging word on the bed covers or briefcase.

Action required: Write an encouraging note on an envelope or a piece of paper, like "Have a great day" or "I love you" and leave it at a place where the receiver can find it easily.

Time needed: 2 minutes.

60. FIND RECREATIONAL OPPORTUNITIES

If you know what you intend to do, it becomes easy to make plans with others. Think about what people close to you like. Thereafter, plan some event together which would be entertaining.

Action required: Browse Google, Twitter or Facebook and find out what's happening in your city in the current week. Is there a free-of-cost event which you can enjoy with your dear ones? Maybe, there is a fundraiser event going on for some local religious work, which you can attend with your sister.

Time needed: 5 minutes.

61. DO SOMETHING FOR SELF-SATISFACTION

If you are not satisfied, it is difficult to find satisfaction in relationships. So, take some time out to do something every day that makes you happy, be it meditating for 3-10 minutes or listening to your favourite song. When we are happy within ourselves, we can give happiness to others. This helps to improve our social life and relationships.

Action required: Which is the smallest task that can make you smile? Spend 5 minutes doing it. The task could be as simple as watching birds chirp while sitting on the veranda, sipping a cup of coffee or writing a journal about your daily routine.

Time needed: 5 minutes.

62. LEARN NEW JOKES

Knowing the art of making people laugh is an excellent way to begin a conversation. It is always considered good to tell a joke as it provides entertainment to people by making them. Moreover, laughing together makes a relationship strong.

Action required: Search for a joke that tickles you on Google. If it makes you laugh, it might make others laugh too. You can either memorize it by reading it a couple of times or write it down to remember it later.

Time needed: 2 minutes.

❑

9

Rest and Leisure

News habits are not just nurtured by self-improvement. You may also make some small changes which are associated with your interests and passions. In this chapter, we shall discuss how we can add fun-filled activities to our life.

63. WAKE UP BEFORE 5.00 AM

"Early to bed and early to rise makes a person healthy, wealthy and wise." This age-old saying is a habit that has been proven to make a person healthy, rich and intelligent.

There is no doubt that there are many benefits to waking up early in the morning. Rising early helps you to exercise, have breakfast and wrap up some pending work before leaving for the office. One-fourth of the world's population loves to rise early, while many prefer to stay up late at night. Research has proved that those who rise early are more cooperative by nature and can analyze any event correctly. In contrast, those who stay up late at night are more imaginative and love to spend more time with their selves.

Research has proved that early risers are self-motivated. They can work longer and they follow directions better. They aim high and make better future plans. They take better care of their health and suffer less from depression than those who stay up late at night.

In contrast, those who work late into the night have better memory and are more intelligent than the early risers. They can work faster and they experiment with new things more with an open mind. Those who remain awake till late in the night may also be as healthy, rich and intelligent as those who rise early.

However, it is logical that rising early is more beneficial. In case you feel like sleeping a bit more, do so.

64. READ A FEW PAGES OF A BOOK

Reading has many benefits. It helps in mental exercise, improves concentration and reduces age-related stress. Moreover, it helps in reducing blood pressure and relieves depression. Informative books enhance your knowledge, improve your analytical ability and offer an opportunity to read something new every day in merely a few minutes.

Action required: If you are not a regular reader, find 5 minutes to read. Reading in the evening is considered beneficial as it helps you get better sleep after a hard day's work. Choose good, easy and informative books to read. 'Amazon' is an excellent place to start as it has the best collection of best-selling books.

Time needed: 5 minutes.

65. STEP OUTDOORS

Spending some time outside your home can work wonders for your physical and mental health. There are several examples to prove that spending time with Nature can reduce stress, give you the strength to fight depression, help you get a night of better sleep and has a positive effect on your overall well-being. A study published in the journal of "Environmental Science and Technology" shows exercising in a 'green' environment can significantly improve your mental and physical health.

Action required: Whenever possible, go outside and get some fresh air. Instead of making tea or watching videos during your spare time, go out and water the plants in the garden and breathe deeply. If you live in a city, spend some time in the sun so that your body could get Vitamin D to improve your overall health.

Time needed: 5 minutes.

66. READ ARTICLES ON WIKIPEDIA

Most children have wonderfully elaborated general knowledge because they are keen on learning and reading about the world around them. As we age, we forget about learning fun-filled activities and only concentrate on learning about important things related to our daily routine. We only concentrate on specific important subjects and forget about expanding the horizons of our knowledge. You can increase your general knowledge by reading one article on Wikipedia every day and become a more interesting person by working sincerely on your habits and ideas.

Action required: There are thought-provoking articles that appear every day on the front page of Wikipedia. There is a lot you can learn by reading an article on Wikipedia, which under ordinary circumstances, you would not bother to read.

Time needed: 1 to 5 minutes, depending on your reading speed and the length of the article.

67. SPARE A WHILE TO HUG A DEAR ONE/ CHILD/PET

Physical contact is essential to develop our skills. Hugging emits a happy hormone called Oxytocin which reduces stress and improves immunity. Physical touch triggers affection and improves communication between couples, parents and children. Hugging is not just confined to lovers – you can get the same satisfaction by hugging a friend, child, lamb or even a pet.

Action required: Hug a person and feel the flow of happy hormones.

Time needed: 1 to 5 minutes (the more the better but even a minute's hug can benefit you).

68. WRITE THREE THINGS YOU ARE THANKFUL TO

"Count your blessings" is a piece of advice given to many but only a few follows it. If you make it a habit to write about three things that you are grateful for in your 'gratitude book' every day, it could change your perspective on life, make you happy, improve your relationships and reduce stress.

Action required: Keep a notepad or diary to jot down things you are grateful for. Before you begin to write, think for a few minutes about three things to which you owe a debt of gratitude. You might think you tend to forget things fast, but the more people think, the more opportunities they get to show how grateful they are. Your three items can be as small or as large as you wish. The actual list makes no difference. It is the process of creation from which you are benefitted.

Time needed: 5 minutes.

69. READ A SUMMARY OF THE DAY'S WORLD NEWS

The happenings of the world around you can impact many spheres of your life. If you are not well aware of global activities, your life is as meaningless as bubbles. Knowledge is power. That is the reason why oppressive regimes often ban their citizens from reading newspapers. North Korea is a present example. Reading the news gives you all the benefits of reading and equips you with relevant information. You will never be short of subjects to discuss.

Action required: Subscribe to a daily newspaper (it could be in a printed form or an e-paper available on your e-mail) or go through a news website. You do not need to read every news item. You can just go through the headlines and read the news that interests you. You need to remember that even the most reputed media house may be biased in their views. It is thus important to form your own opinion.

Time needed: 5 minutes.

70. LEARN A NEW WORD

Expanding your vocabulary, be it in your first language or second, has many benefits. Expanding your vocabulary

will bring about a remarkable improvement in your communication skills. With a little practice, you can increase your self-confidence in social situations. Learning a new language can seem like a daunting task but if you are sincere enough to learn a new word every day, you will be surprised at how easily you have improved your vocabulary.

Action required: Make a list of new words from a dictionary or subscribe to "One Word A Day" (OWAD). Its mailing lists are available on language-learning websites. If you are trying to learn a new language, acquire a list of words that are used widely. This will help you improve your communication skills in the new language you are learning.

Time needed: 2 minutes.

71. INDULGE IN A SUDDEN ACT OF KINDNESS

Most people spend their lives fulfilling their desires and needs. However, it is difficult to attain true happiness with such a self-serving perspective. Helping others in small ways can provide a lot of mental peace and if you involve yourself in acts of kindness regularly, you will earn yourself a lot of happiness over time.

Action required: Identify small acts of kindness which can bring a smile to others, and incorporate them into your daily routine. For instance, putting some money into the parking meter if you see its time limit coming to an end, vacating your seat on a bus or train for an elderly person or pregnant lady or donating an unused commodity for some charitable purpose.

Time needed: 1 to 5 minutes.

72. LISTEN TO A POPULAR SONG

Music has a strong influence on your mind. Listening to a good song can give you immense pleasure, reduce stress, increase productivity and even improve your physical health.

Action required: Tune in to your favourite track or listen to upbeat songs on social music sites like 'Mood Booster.' Go through the list of songs. Play them and sing along.

Time needed: 4 minutes.

73. LISTEN TO TED TALKS OR WATCH MOTIVATIONAL VIDEOS

Some people can rise above books and curricula and motivate us with new ideas and perspectives. TED introduce us to the motivational lectures of many visionary leaders of our times and sites like Upworthy and YouTube is full of motivational and captivating videos. A good video not only provides entertainment but also influences your entire life's philosophy.

Action required: Listen to TED talks through the ted.com website or through the TED app, where many inspirational conversations are enlisted under different categories. Listen to a conversation of less than 10-minute duration. You need to limit your viewing time as you can easily spend hours on these sites once you indulge in them.

Time needed: 1 to 5 minutes.

74. STEP OUT OF YOUR COMFORT ZONE

Can you propel yourself to the peak of success in one go? A painstaking task may cause a little difficulty, but it can enormously enhance your self-confidence and open new doors of opportunity for you to try new tasks that you have never thought you could do before.

Action required: There are many small tasks which you can start by stepping out of your comfort zone –

- Add variations to your daily routine. Take a different route to work or watch a documentary instead of your usual drama.

- Try something innovative like new food, new music or a new style of exercise.
- Do something that you dread, like making monotonous calls to prospective customers, signing up for a class or conversing with a stranger.

Time needed: 1 to 5 minutes.

75. MAKE A CARTOON OR SKETCH

Most children love to create something, but we adults are too involved in making our own designs. We often label our work as "good" or "not creative" and never pick up the pencil for the second time. A small creative task like making a quick doodle or sketch is like a game to your mind. This habit can prove to have healing effects, reduce stress, inspire creativity and also enhance your productivity and concentration along the way.

❑

10

Organization

Never underestimate the benefits of being organized. To be honest, I feel I am a bit lazy, but doing a bit of cleaning and other chores helps me to tidy up and focus on what's important. Moreover, it is important to know where your shoes are before going on a regular run.

You need not feel bored at the idea of organizing things. Overall, you need to spend merely 15 to 30 minutes every day to create a clean living/working environment. Let us discuss some habits which will help you organize.

76. FIX YOUR BROKEN WINDOWS

You may not have broken windows, but there are little things which, if ignored, could increase your stress levels. Some common 'broken windows' are:

- Dirty utensils kept in the sink basin.

- Random junk mails.
- Dirty or unkempt clothes.
- Cluttered kitchen.
- Garbage that needs to be discarded.

Action required: Having completed the required tasks, your next task would depend on how you may want to feel afterwards. If you want to begin the day in an organized way, then give this habit the first priority on your work list. Do this at the end of the day with a sense of satisfaction when you prepare to go to bed.

Think about those areas of your home which make you feel irritated or tense. Most of these areas can be fixed in minutes. Even then, we can ignore them and allow peace to prevail at the back of the mind. Having paid attention to your broken windows, you will notice a marked decrease in stress levels. Try this on various other things like 'broken windows.'

Time needed: 5 minutes.

77. LOOK FOR SOMETHING YOU CAN SELL (OR DISCARD)

This is a good way to save or earn money. The money you get in the process of selling something can be used to pay bills or buy groceries. Marketing worthless things can do away with the problem of paying for something. Moreover, you earn money and get rid of worthless things. You create space in your home and feel good at having helped others. Decorating or cleaning your home helps you avoid buying things which spread filth and dirt.

Action required: Place all the goods that you want to sell, market or discard in a box or dustbin. Look for things every day that fall into these three categories and place them in the boxes. Look for an opportunity throughout the day to sell them.

Time needed: 2 minutes.

78. ARRANGE YOUR BED PROPERLY

If you start your day by arranging your bed, you will surely have a good day. It is an important habit because a bed that is neatly arranged looks organized. Moreover, instead of hunting for a pillow and blanket, relaxing on a tidy bed comes as a reward.

Action required: Remove the bed sheet, mattress and pillow from your bed. If you see some useless things lying around, remove them too. Dust off your bed sheet and pillow and place them properly on the mattress.

Time needed: 2 minutes.

79. CLEAN YOUR DRESSING TABLE

A tidy countertop or dressing table means less clatter and stress. It is important to keep such places clean because we are habitual to throwing clothes, magazines and other things on them and forget to remove them.

Action required: Lift the dresser-top or countertop and if you find any unrelated things on top of them, put them in their appropriate places. If you find anything useless, then put that thing into the dustbin. If you find something recyclable, then put that thing in the recycle bin. Until the whole place is cleaned up, keep repeating the process.

Time needed: 5 minutes.

80. DO THREE THINGS

There are some simple things you can do every day to keep your home or office clean and tidy. This saves you the trouble of tidying up things if you were to clean your home or office in a week or month. One way to do this is to determine a fixed place for everything and put everything back in its place after completing the day's work.

Action required: Identify three things which are not in their place. Once you have identified them, put them back in their place. If you haven't decided on a fixed place for them, then store them in a store room.

Time needed: 3 minutes.

81. CLEAN ONE THING AT A TIME

If your home or office is clean, you would not want to make it filthy. It is easy to clean one thing at a time you certainly would be able to gradually clean up your entire home or office. Keeping things clean is a must-have habit as it helps you remain organized and improves your hygiene habits.

Action required: Select any one thing to clean in your home or office. It could be a drawer in your desk, your furniture or even your garbage bin. Assemble the things you need for cleaning and get down to the job.

Time needed: 5 minutes.

82. SIGN UP FOR A PAPERLESS INITIATIVE

The less paper you have at your home or in the office, the less garbage you would have to clean and the easier it would be for you to remain organized. It may be considered a bonus because less use of paper is beneficial for the environment.

Action required: Make a list of companies that send you monthly bills and statements. Ask them for a paperless communication or request by going to their websites.

Time needed: 3 minutes.

83. MAKE A FILE OF RECEIPTS, POSTS AND BILLS

If you keep filing receipts, letters and bills, you can avoid scattering papers here and there and get more organized.

Daily filing of paper will keep your counter and other places clean. Additionally, it will be easier to search for a particular paper when you need it.

Action required: Assemble all your receipts, posts and bills. Sort them to see which you need to keep and those that can be discarded. Then, file them according to their sender and date. Tear up those that you do not need or recycle them.

Time needed: 4 minutes.

84. DISCARD SOME OF THE THINGS

Dust often spreads through things that we neither use nor discard. Some things are better to be thrown into the waste bin than be on your desk or counter. Broken items or overused items take up much of your precious space. Once you throw away such things, you could have space to accommodate new things in their place.

Action required: Search for something which is of no use to you. Broken or irreparable things or those which you have already utilized should be discarded or recycled. One thumb rule is that anything you haven't used for six months is unlikely to be used for the next six months.

Time needed: 2 minutes.

85. CLEAN UP YOUR DIGITAL JUNK

Junk exists not just in your home or office, but also in your computer. It is important to consider this carefully because even this junk can be distracting to you.

Action required: Login to your computer, clear desktop icons, organize documents in folders and put the files you do not need into the recycle bin. Before completing this task, make sure to clear your recycle bin.

Time needed: 5 minutes.

86. CHECK FOR EXPIRED FOOD AND COUPONS

Expired food items and coupons are of no value to you and are just taking up space. Discarding such things can clear up space and save you from consuming stale food items. This habit can also save you from stress and ailments.

Action required: Search your refrigerator, kitchen and cupboards for food items that have crossed their date of expiration and discard them immediately. Then search your purse for expired coupons. If six months have lapsed after the coupons' date of expiry, discard them. If not, you can send them to foreign military families. To learn how to make packets from expired coupons and to send such coupons to foreign military bases, visit http://www.ocpnet.org

Time needed: 4 minutes.

87. DETERMINE FIXED PLACES TO STORE ITEMS

If we are disorganized, it is because there is no proper system of storing things inside our homes. The best way to get rid of all junk is by determining definite places for everything that you bring with you as you enter your home.

Action required: Think of the goods you would carry to your workplace, gym or any other activities. Then think of fixed places for all the goods which you intend to take with you. Generally, these goods include car keys, purses, laptops, briefcases, shoes, books, coins, mobile phones and clothes to wear at the gym. Take a few minutes to put these in their fixed places.

Time needed: 5 minutes.

88. ASSEMBLE ALL DIRTY LINEN

Scattered dirty linen in your home gives it an impression of being more disorganized than it actually is. So, assemble them and put them into their right place which is the washing machine. You might have heaps of dirty linen near the washing machine. So, wash only a fixed number of clothes that can be dried easily. The rest can be kept in a basket to be washed later.

Action required: Take a round of your home and assemble all dirty linen. Put them all in a basket and place them near the washing machine.

Time needed: 3 minutes.

89. CHECK FOR REPLACEABLE OR REPAIRABLE THINGS

To be organized, you need to know the things in your home which can be changed, else what is the point in changing your toilet paper after the situation has worsened?

Action required: Check your household items like toilet paper, paper towels, diapers, garbage bags and light bulbs. Before buying new items, ensure that you have a sufficient quantity of all these necessary items. If something is missing, write it down on your shopping list before leaving the house for shopping.

Time needed: 4 minutes.

90. CLEAN A SURFACE

Dirt and dust create filth. Cleaning one surface at a time helps you get rid of filth and each surface becomes clean. You certainly wouldn't want to mess up a clean surface.

Action required: Choose a dresser-top, desktop or table-top to clean. Use your all-purpose cleaner, scrubber or paper towel to clean them. Make sure to clean the edges too while cleaning surfaces so that no dirt remains in them.

Time needed: 2 minutes.

91. UTILIZE THE RECYCLE BIN

The more things you have in your recycle bin, the less filth would you have in your home or office. Recycle bins help in clearing unwanted papers and also help the environment to remain clean. Recycling bins clear paper filth, helps you get organized and encourage you to put less waste material in landfills.

Action required: Put all the unwanted paper in your home or office into the waste bin. All used boxes, soup or vegetable pouches and plastic plates collected in the waste bin can be put into the recycle bin.

Time needed: 2 minutes.

❑

11

Health and Physical Fitness

There is unfortunately no way to improve your physical health by investing only 5 minutes. You need to devote a minimum of 30 minutes for this purpose.

All you can do with the help of a "Micro Habits" daily routine is to make small changes in support of your goal to improve your overall health and physical fitness. This way, when you exercise or sit for your meal, you can reap maximum benefits from every activity. To help you get started, here are some suggestions.

92. CHECK YOUR WEIGHT EVERY DAY

This is not something you will love to hear, but by checking your weight every day, you will be able to set clear health goals. It is important to know that your weight may

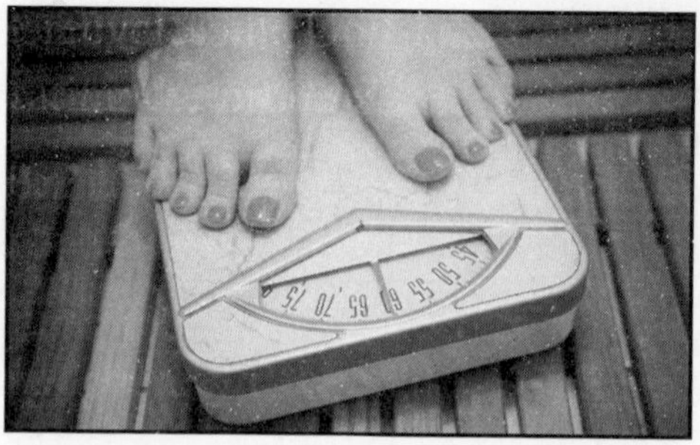

increase or decrease daily. So, if you notice a hike in your weight for a day or two, you need to panic. To get correct results, immediately examine your weight. The website http://bit.ly/1pPmKII has an article which tells you why you should examine your weight every morning.

Action required: This is very simple. Buy a weighing machine and keep it in an important place, like your bathroom. Check your weight regularly every day and make a note of it in your diary.

Time needed: Less than 1 minute.

93. USE SKIPPING ROPE FOR MORNING EXERCISE

Starting your day with exercise will immediately lift your mood. It may not be initially easy to exercise first thing in the morning, but once you get used to it, your body will wait impatiently for some physical movement every morning.

If you cannot go to a gym every morning, skipping rope is an ideal alternative. An intense session of skipping rope has many benefits. It is a complete physical exercise which helps in blood circulation. It puts less pressure on your joints than walking.

Action required: After moving out of bed in the morning, listen to your favourite song and start skipping. Try not to stop in the midst of skipping. Once you master this skill, any obstruction will go away. Keep skipping till the end of the song. Once the song ends, stop and begin your daily routine.

Time needed: 5 minutes.

94. MAKE A DIET BOOK

This is probably another thing you don't want to do, but to reduce weight and maintain you need to do this. Maintaining a diet book will help you get a concrete idea of what you are eating and how much you are eating. You will be surprised to see your daily intake.

A diet book is effective, because it makes you accountable towards your meals, is a physical representation of your daily eating habits, encourages you to avoid snacking and helps you to achieve your health goals. At first sight, this habit may trigger negative thoughts, but you will soon be proud of yourself for keeping an account of your meals.

Action required: Download a tool like 'My Fitness Pal' which will help you track your calories. Make a habit of writing down everything that you consume for meals and snacks and as part of your "Micro Habits" daily routine, put all your information in your diet book. If you face any difficulty in remembering what you have eaten in your meals, implement this habit twice a day, once in the morning and once in the evening.

Time needed: 4 minutes.

95. CLEAN THE WIPES WITH BOILING WATER

Technically speaking, this habit could be part of your combined routine, but this is an activity which can influence your health and the health of your family as well. Studies have proved that your kitchen wipe is the most germ-infected commodity in your home. It is something that is used to clean the oiliness left behind by raw meat on your kitchen cabinet, stale food and other scattered things. These things can spread harmful bacteria. The easiest solution to this problem is to clean the wipes in boiling water in a microwave.

Action required: This is an easy habit which can be included in the evening daily routine. Soak the wipes in water, put them in a utensil and boil them in a microwave. Make sure you wear gloves before you wring the wipes dry. You can get rid of most germs including bacteria through this method.

Time needed: 1 minute.

96. MAKE A COOL ANTIOXIDANT DRINK

If you want instant energy, prepare and drink a cool antioxidant drink. Such drinks have many vitamins and minerals and to have such a drink in a day would infuse you with energy.

Action required: There are tons of delicious antioxidant drink recipes on the Internet. So, search for such a recipe or two on Google. If you want to know about one such recipe right now, here's how to make one which is my personal favourite:

- A cup of cool berry mix (it usually includes litchi, red cherry, pomegranate, raspberry and blueberry)
- 4 ounces of fat-free curd
- A cup of almond milk
- Two tablespoons of fine fibres
- Two ice cubes

Mix all the ingredients and churn until you get a smooth consistency. Add ice cubes according to your preference. It tastes really good and will satisfy even the most senior members of your family. If you are in a hurry, you can keep it in a travel cup and enjoy it while on your way to work or school.

Time needed: 5 minutes.

97. CLEAN YOUR TONGUE

You read it right. Along with daily brushing and flossing your teeth, it is important to clean your tongue too. This is an important habit as bacteria keep accumulating at the back of your tongue which causes bad breath.

Action required: After brushing your teeth, clean your tongue back and forth with your brush. The trick is that you can do this without the normal gargling and rinsing. Brush your tongue slowly until you feel a stretch.

Time needed: 2 minutes.

98. TAKE VITAMINS EVERY DAY

It is essential for everyone to take vitamins daily. If you will take vitamins daily, you will have a good day. Vitamins are essential to strengthen your immune system, increase alertness and help your body get the essential nutrients it required.

Action required: This habit can be made effective with the help of a diet book. Jot down all the nutrients you consume in a week and find out which essential nutrients you are missing. There are some online nutrition tools available like 'Fit Day' which will tell you if you are deficient in essential vitamins even if you are taking the recommended amount. If you are not taking the necessary amount of essential vitamins, then purchase essential vitamin supplements that match your age and nutritional needs. To know more about suitable vitamins, read the WebMD article on the website http://www.webmd.com/diet/features/what-vitamin-should-i-take

Time needed: Less than 1 minute.

99. CONSUME PUDINA (MINT)

Other than refreshing your breath, pudina leaves (mint) can improve your memory power and alertness, and acts as a natural stimulant.

You can make use of mint in many ways. How you would use it will depend on its properties. You can either consume it or apply it on the skin according to the instruction of a physician.

Action required: You can drink it as a coolant, chew flavoured mint chewing gum, brush your teeth with mint-flavoured toothpaste or rub a few drops of peppermint-rich oil under your nostrils. All in all, you can use it according to your needs.

Time needed: Less than 1 minute.

100. MEDITATE

Meditation is a process of concentrating your mind on a particular thing (like your breath or the sound of waves) and removing the obstructing elements. It has been proved that meditation reduces stress and enhances creativity, concentration and memory.

Some people meditate for hours during the evening, while others spend a few minutes meditating in the morning. I suggest you begin by meditating for a few minutes in the morning. If you enjoy it, you may increase the time limit. By doing it for a few minutes every day, you will notice its wonderful benefits.

Action required: Find a quiet and secluded place away from all distractions. Set the timer for a duration of 5 minutes so that you do not take much time and your mind does not become impatient. Start by taking a deep breath and disposing of your stress. Flex your muscles so that you may feel relaxed from within. Remove all thoughts from your mind and only think about the present moment. Initially, you might feel a bit frustrated. If this happens, concentrate on your breaths and do away with all the depressing thoughts. Concentrate on different body parts so that you may know the point where your concentration stabilizes.

Time needed: 5 minutes.

101. EAT NUTRITIOUS FOOD

You cannot merely survive on a liquid diet. There are plenty of other food items which can be taken for breakfast

and which can improve your work performance. Prepare (or pack) a healthy meal for positive uplift for the rest of the day.

Action required: What you cook to eat depends on your personal preferences, but some suggestions to get you started are: a small bowl of berries, a breakfast bar without sugar, yoghurt with granola or legumes, or fibre-rich bread with an egg. All these alternatives are healthy and easy to acquire. Do not eat the same food every day as your body may get accustomed to it. It is always beneficial to try new foods.

Time needed: 1 to 5 minutes.

Practice all 101 habits together

You are now acquainted with 101 small changes that can be included in your "Micro Habits" daily routine. As you have noticed, they are mostly ones which take very less time to complete. You'll do each of the tasks in one day. It is important to make a daily routine which focuses on essential areas.

Now, it is time to transform information into action. In the next section, you will get to know how during the creation of a "Micro Habits" daily routine, you can choose a routine which will give you the maximum benefits in the minimum time. Come, let us move on to the next section.

❑

12

8 Phases of Making "Micro Habits" Daily Routine

"Micro Habits" is about sticking to a daily routine rather than individual habits. You tend to automatically gravitate towards one thing after another without thinking about each element. This is the reason why you should develop the habit of following a daily routine.

You can implement your habits without hesitation because we know the ways to create a power-packed "Micro Habits" daily routine. Your life starts to change with the newly-created daily routine. When you complete your day impeccably with the help the of "Micro Habits" daily routine, you make improvements in multiple spheres of your life.

Choosing personal habits and completing the daily routine may be a little boring. However, do not worry. This section will discuss the creation of a daily routine in eight phases, which will not tire or bore you. You will get to know which habits are more effective for you and how they can be made functional in your daily routine.

PHASE 1: SELECT THE TIME AND PLACE

All the "Micro Habits" daily focus on a particular time and place of the day. Some examples and ideas of time and place are given here which you may select to begin building a daily routine.

At home in the morning

To complete "Micro Habits" and start your day with productive thoughts, the best place is your home and the best time is in the morning. Consider all work that you can complete at home before leaving for work and include them in your daily routine. The example of arranging your bed in the morning and packing your lunch can be cited. Such work keeps your home organized, prepares you for the day and gives you the chance of walking into a clean and tidy home in the evening for rest.

The first part of the working day in the office

What would you like to do immediately after reaching the office? If you are motivated and full of energy right at the start of the working day, then it is the best time and the office is the best place for a "Micro Habits" daily routine.

After being seated in the office, making a list of all important work to be done on that day, arranging the scattered documents and cleaning up your desk and computer are three habits you may consider carefully. This daily routine will assist you in organizing the rest of the day and starting the day with productive thoughts.

Ending your working day in the office

Ending your working day with the "Micro Habits" daily routine is good because it is good to end your day with positive thoughts. After working for the entire day, the end-of-the-day daily routine gives you the last chance to feel satisfied.

One good habit of ending a day's work is to mark out all-important tasks for the next day. This will help you have practical knowledge of the next day's tasks which needs to be done when you reach the office.

At home in the evening

The time between reaching home after work in the evening and after becoming relaxed upon reaching home is the best time for "Micro Habits." This is a very useful time as allows it you to prepare for the following day's work. The evening is the best time for habits like preparing lunch for the next day and checking your posts.

While working out in the gym

The gym is a good option to be included in the "Micro Habits" daily routine. Having determined a time for exercise in your daily routine, allows you to do an effective practice in the least possible time. A consistent practice of doing one exercise after another will result in great improvement.

For instance, you can include habits like stretching, meditation, consuming healthy drinks and examining your weight. All these can be done within 10 to 15 minutes after exercise and weight-lifting.

During a journey or on the road

Even if you are on the road, you can make the "Micro Habits" daily routine. Many tasks can be completed while you are in a car, bus or train on your daily commute. Install Bluetooth in your car. Call a friend or family member with whom you haven't spoken in the recent past. While travelling for 30 minutes by train back home, you can make a list of things to be done the next day or respond to unanswered written messages received during the day. This is the time you can complete small tasks, lest the time goes waste.

During lunch

You have enough time during lunch break to complete a task. Since you are in a productive mood during working hours, your daily routine proceeds naturally. Instead of wasting a span of 30 minutes to one hour of lunch break at the lunch room or canteen, you can bring some changes in your life. There are a lot of things you can do during this time. You can introduce yourself to a new person, check your bank account balance or do a 5-minute meditation to retain your concentration for the rest of the day.

PHASE 2: MAKE ONE DAILY ROUTINE AT A TIME

There are different views on how much time it takes to form new habits. Some people say one week, some 21 days and for others, it takes 3 months. It is not important how much time you spend on a habit. It is more important to concentrate on one habit at a time.

You can't include too many routines at the same time. The process is so complex that your willpower will revolt if you were to put too much pressure on yourself. In other words, you will not be able to sustain it for a long time.

Let us consider toning down our expectations in support of this step. Low expectations mean one's inability to limit one's feelings, thoughts and actions. In other words, our willpower is like a muscle which tires out due to continuous work. We all have our own limits of willpower and once exhausted, it is difficult to stay concentrated.

The purpose of concentrating on one routine at a time is to avoid tiring out our willpower so that we do not feel tired or bored. My suggestion is that before adding a new habit or change, concentrate on one habit for at least a month.

PHASE 3: START WITH 'SMALL WINS'

This book lists 101 habits in all. As far as habits are concerned, when you start with simple habits like taking vitamin tablets as part of your daily routine, you will feel like learning a new art and it will be easier to consider your next habit.

My suggestion is that you observe the seven different categories of small changes. Look for habits which are short and simple and would take 1 to 3 minutes to complete. Until you make one "Micro Habits" daily routine, just concentrate on these easy habits. Once this is done, you are free to change or swap habits and through your personal goals, you can bring small changes in your routine.

PHASE 4: MAKE A LOGICAL CHECKLIST

We have discussed the checklists earlier. Your checklist should have a combination of habits and important tasks that needs to be completed. All habits should be put together and they should be seamlessly intertwined.

To maintain progress in the checklist of habits, movement from one chamber to another is important. Your checklist can be printed, written or stored in an application. Remember, applications are very useful in undertaking this work.

PHASE 5: SPECIFY 'REASON'

There are many reasons why you may quit a new habit. Some quit due to a negative influence or feeling of pain. Others find a habit difficult and quit because of fear of criticism. To quit habits like arranging the bed or making a daily budget is easy. However, if you want long-term and positive life changes, you need to find new ways to follow a new daily routine.

To ensure that you do not quit the "Micro Habits" daily routine, you need to specify the reason behind every individual task. The reason must be important and practical. Some people adopt "Micro Habits" daily routines for longevity, while others adopt them to spend more time with their family. There are thousands of reasons, but you need to identify the most important reasons as to why you want to complete the "Micro Habits" daily routine.

PHASE 6: BE ACCOUNTABLE

To avoid doing something is obviously easier than doing it. For instance, relaxing on the sofa is far easier than exercising. However, such relaxation will help you get no benefit. Many fail to complete the "Micro Habits" daily routine because they find it easy to quit. So, you need to be accountable publicly to follow the "Micro Habits" daily routine.

Making your progress public on social media, telling your friends or family members about your daily routine and using your phone alarm to begin your daily routine are some ways and alternatives available to you.

In the past, the 'Lift' app has proved to be very useful for me, as it helped me to maintain and follow my daily routine habits. It is like keeping an excellent trainer in your pocket.

By including it as a habit, you can examine it regularly after completion of the "Micro Habits" daily routine and also remain accountable to it. Believe me, you must understand that informing people about your progress provides enough motivation in following the "Micro Habits" daily routine.

PHASE 7: DETERMINE SMALL AND ENJOYABLE REWARDS

Completing the "Micro Habits" daily routine is nothing less than an achievement, which should be rewarded. Howsoever small is the reward, it has a long-term and positive effect and acts as a motivator in completing the daily routine. You can reward yourself by watching a film late in the night or give some healthy reward every day for a month.

PHASE 8: BE MINDFUL OF REPETITION

Repetition is the key to the "Micro Habits" daily routine for the first month. Even if you have to postpone a habit or two for some reason, it is mandatory to follow the daily routine. Your muscles get accustomed to the routine and they remember that the routine has to be followed every day.

If you miss following the routine on a certain day, there is no harm. It happens to everyone. However, it is important to remember that you do not miss it on two consecutive days and if any task is left undone on a day, at least a part of it must be completed the next day.

The stronger and more developed your "Micro Habits" daily routine is, the more benefits you will get. A routine is a route to bring positive changes in your life. A good daily routine is like a beneficial casket attached to your life.

Even the best of daily routines can face hindrances. It is not surprising that you might have to quit your daily routine due to an unexpected incident. Fortunately, you have the knowledge to tackle such a situation. Since knowledge is power, it is important to know the ways to tackle common drawbacks of the "Micro Habits" daily routine. The more you know about the elements of the "Micro Habits" daily routine, the more successful you would be.

❑

13

Two Examples of "Micro Habits" Daily Routine

By this time, you must have read about many suggestions and ideas. There is a possibility that you still have not understood the "Micro Habits" daily routine in detail. If you are like me, some specific examples might help you understand it better. This is the reason that this section has been designed to show you how to transform information into action.

I have included two kinds of daily routines. The first is the 'ordinary' morning routine which includes the habits which may bring many improvements in your life. The second routine focuses on a 'special' area of productivity.

We use it for determining where and how we should allocate our limited time and energy.

Lastly, I would request you to consider carefully why you should be doing each individual task. Generally speaking, why do you do any work? If you do not have a good impression about a work, you would not possibly be doing it.

Example 1: 'Ordinary morning "Micro Habits" daily routine.

Total time: Less than 10 minutes.

1. Arrange your bed in the morning. (**Reason:** I work from home and I need to keep the environment of my home productive.)
2. I examine my weight in the bathroom. (**Reason:** I am a competitive marathon runner. tor to give a good performance, I need to maintain my weight. Daily examination of weight will help me concentrate on my goal.)
3. I clean my face with warm water and cleanser. (**Reason:** Studies show that washing your face in the morning helps you feel awake and energetic.)
4. I go to the kitchen and drink 2 glasses of cold water with lemon in it. (**Reason:** Lemon helps you feel awake. Moreover, out of the necessary eight doses of daily water intake, I get two immediately.)
5. I take vitamins every day. (**Reason:** Most food items lack nutritious elements. Following a rule of

daily vitamin intake helps me remember what I am missing in my dosage.)

6. I prepare an energetic drink. I mix up various recipes but I prefer the ones that have protein, potassium and antioxidants in them. (**Reason:** This simple drink helps me remain energetic for the rest of the day).
7. I send love letters to my lover. (**Reason:** Small acts done daily are the key to a successful relationship.)
8. Along with developing my habits, I update my mobile phone apps. (**Reason:** To bring long-term improvements, you need to search for new habits on the daily basis.) For tracking, I prefer the "Lift" app. which is available at http://lift.do

Example 2: Productivity "Micro Habits" daily routine.

Total time: 10 to 15 minutes.

1. I review my quarterly goals. (**Reason:** Daily review of my quarterly aims helps me stay concentrated on my important plans.)
2. I search for the 100 best books, both priced and free of cost on Kindle. (**Reason:** From the business point-of-view, it is important to know what is selling most in the market at present).
3. I mark out my three most important tasks. (**Reason:** When I look at the long list of tasks to be done during the week, I try to focus on some big tasks each day.)

4. Map the steps that need to be taken in some key areas of each plan. (**Reason:** I need to be really strict with the most important tasks. Instead of writing false reports like "work in next book," I prefer to write my actual deliverables.)

5. I clear my desktop. (**Reason:** I like to work on a well-arranged desktop. This helps me remain focused on my real goals and I do not get distracted.)

6. I begin with the toughest task. (**Reason:** As we have already discussed, if you complete the most difficult task first, the other tasks of the day do not seem difficult. My preliminary work starts with some kind of writing.)

7. I set my Pomodoro for my first task. (**Reason:** I like to work in phases. I make use of the Pomodoro amplified edition to write in 25 to 50-minute blocks. For me, this is the way of staying focused on the task at hand.)

How to make your "Micro Habits" daily routine

There are two kinds of daily routines. The first is a mixed compilation of the works of different areas of your life. The second sheds light on the improvement of specific long-term achievement. Which is best for you will depend on your specific situation.

I suggest you take a close look at your life and select one area that needs to be improved the most.

Do you find it difficult to go to a trench early in the morning? If so, the solution lies in an energising morning routine.

Are you struggling to fulfil all your goals at work? If so, then the productivity routine will be helpful for you.

Do you often waste a lot of time before going to bed at night? Then the evening routine will be the most beneficial for you.

As I have said earlier, the best benefit of the "Micro Habits" routine can be had by developing a routine of following the same habit for a few weeks. If you follow one routine comfortably, then you can add another routine to your day. As long as you are implementing dozens of minor changes every day, you can explore and repeat them over and over again without wasting a lot of your time.

Now I admit that this is the ideal approach to "Micro Habits." On a more realistic plane, I would want each of your tasks to be completed properly. I am well aware that your routine shall often face challenges and hindrances. So, it is important to plan beforehand so that you know what to do should such situations arise.

Come, let us discuss this in the next section.

❑

14

Hindrances and Challenges of "Micro Habits" Routine: What to Do?

Habits usually start logically well. You get curious about a new routine and would wish to bring changes in your life. You would make your routine and see the immediate positive impacts. However, something or the other will keep happening in your life which causes hindrances for you. If you are forced to stop following your routine for one reason or another, you should have some plan to tackle the hindrances. Holidays, ailments and emergencies are usually the reasons which could hinder the routine.

People usually do not quit the routine due to lethargy. External activities derail their efforts for a few days. A few days without completing the routine turns into weeks and people do not understand how to start again. If this is happening to you, fortunately, there are some ways to stop it.

Strategy 1: Prepare an alternative plan

It is a fact that there will be hindrances in the way of your routine. Since such hindrances are expected, one should not be discouraged by them and accept them. You need not consider yourself answerable for these hindrances and you should move ahead. You might have to stop your routine for a few days, but instead of getting angry with yourself for the interruption, you should convert the anger into inspiration and complete the routine the next day.

One of the main examples of hindrance is holidays. It can hinder your routine because once you go out for holidays, you neither have the place to follow your routine nor do you have the time. An alternative plan helps you to get over this hindrance and allows you to make the routine a success.

Alternative planning is also known as the implementation concept which identifies the factors that make up your routine. When such obstructive elements emerge, you must make a plan to deal with them.

Let's say, for instance, I suggest you check your bank account statement regularly. However, what if your Internet connectivity is too weak on a particular day? Do you have an alternative plan? If you cannot view your bank account balance Online, call up the customer care number of the bank and enquire about the balance.

Strategy 2: Know the motivational elements

To make an alternative plan, you need to know the elements of motivation. Know your bad habits and such elements of distraction which cast a negative influence on the "Micro Habits" routine. Identifying your bad habits will help you develop your routine. You may want to adopt a healthy lifestyle but habitually eat junk food. When this happens, you need to realise that it is a bad habit which sets you on the path to harm.

For instance, do you eat fast food while skipping your meals? Maybe, you eat fast food only when you feel depressed or sad. These are the elements of motivation you need to identify so that you can make an alternative plan and put aside your negative thoughts. Think of it this way – if I have a healthy and fulfilling lunch, I will not feel hungry in the evening and will not have to step into a fast-food outlet.

Alternative plans help you suppress bad habits and develop good ones, but what if you are not able to stop yourself from quitting the "Micro Habits" routine in one go?

Come, let us look at the larger picture: Not just a habit or two, think about what would happen if you leave the entire routine. Should this happen, you should be aware of how to start the routine all over again.

Strategy 3: Lower all your expectations

There is a fine line between the pressure required to complete a task and the excessive pressure exerted on oneself. Excessive pressure casts a negative influence which you would obviously not want.

Instead of taking up more work than is practical and trying to complete it, it is advisable to concentrate on less workload and only concentrate on executing the most important habits. Do keep this in mind while making your "Micro Habits" daily routine. I have realised that it is easier to complete more work during an emergency. However, if you fill your plate with more than it can hold, some of the contents are bound to spill over.

Strategy 4: Restart with a small routine

The beginning can be discouraging, but it is essential when it comes to the "Micro Habits" routine. If you want to make a new beginning, start with a small routine. To bring the routine on track, start by concentrating on some small habits. The smaller your habit, the better you can start and complete it.

Instead of focusing on the longevity of the routine, look at the small achievements and try to stick to the routine. When you get a proper hold on your routine, you may include more habits in it. Never forget that you should not miss more than one routine in a day.

❑❑❑